The KidHaven Science Library

Cells

by Jeanne DuPrau

You are a child of the universe,
No less than the trees and stars:
You have a right to be here.
And whether or not it is clear to you,
No doubt the universe is unfolding as it should.
—Max Ehrmann

BELOVED DEVIN
OCTOBER 27, 1964 – MARCH 17, 2000

The Devin Shafron Memorial Book Fund

KidHaven Press

KidHaven Press, an imprint of Gale Group, Inc.
10911 Technology Place, San Diego, CA 92127

On cover: Red blood cells with hepatitis virus.

Library of Congress Cataloging-in-Publication Data
DuPrau, Jeanne.
    Cells / by Jeanne DuPrau.
        p. ; cm. — (The KidHaven Science library)
    Includes bibliographical references and index.
    Summary: Discusses the discovery of cells, their functions, cell
    division, the workings of the immune system, and the future of
    cell research.
    ISBN 0-7377-0647-3 (hardback : alk. paper)
    1. Cells—Juvenile literature. [1. Cells.]
    [DNLM: 1. Cells—Juvenile Literature 2. Cell Physiology—
    Juvenile Literature. QH 582.5 D942c 2001] I. Title. II. The
    KidHaven Science library (San Diego, Calif.)
    QH582.5 .D87 2002

    571.6—dc21
    00-012806

Picture Credits for *Cells*

Cover photo: ©Ellen Going Jacobs/The Image Bank
Biological Images, 17, 28
© Kit Kittle/Corbis, 31
National Institute of Health, 25, 36, 40
© Charles O'Rear/Corbis, 10
PhotoDisc, 39, 41
© Robert Pickett/Corbis, 12
Martha Schierholz, 4, 15, 18, 21, 27
© Mark L. Stephenson/Corbis, 19
© John Stevens/FPG International, 22, 33
© The Telegraph Colour Library/FPG International, 7, 8, 35
© V.I. Lab E.R.I.C./FPG International, 13, 37

Copyright 2002 by KidHaven Press, an imprint of Gale Group, Inc.
    10911 Technology Place, San Diego, CA 92127

Contents

Introduction 4

Chapter 1
Life's Building Blocks 6

Chapter 2
How a Cell Works 14

Chapter 3
Cells Make More Cells 24

Chapter 4
Cells in Health and Illness 32

Glossary 43

For Further Exploration 45

Index 47

On a day in 1665, Robert Hooke, a scientist, looked down through the lens of his microscope and saw something that surprised him. He had decided that day to inspect a thin slice of cork. Under the microscope, the slice of cork appeared to be made up of tiny spaces surrounded by walls, a little like a beehive. Hooke later made a drawing of what he had seen.

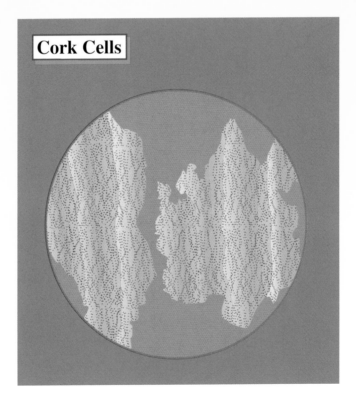

Cork Cells

He thought the spaces in the cork looked like little rooms. They reminded him of the small, plain rooms that monks lived in, which were called cells. So he gave the name "cells" to what he saw in the slice of cork.

Robert Hooke had discovered plant cells. He was probably the first person to see them, and he gave them the name they are still called today. The cells he saw were empty because the piece of cork was no longer a living part of the oak tree it came from. So Hooke didn't realize, on that day in 1665, that he was looking at something that had been alive—something basic not just to plant life, but to all life.

Chapter 1

Life's Building Blocks

Everything alive is made of cells. A pine tree, a goldfish, a beetle, a robin, a human being—all of them are made of cells. The cell is the basic unit of life.

As Robert Hooke saw, a cell is like a tiny room. But there is a big difference between a cell and a room. A cell can move and change shape. It can eat and turn its food into energy. It can reproduce itself. In the tiny "room" of the cell, all the work of life is done.

The Size of a Cell

A few kinds of cells are large enough to see easily. All eggs, for instance, are single cells. They have a cell wall—the shell—and within the wall are the ingredients of life. Chicken eggs, frog eggs, ant eggs, robin eggs—all of them are cells. The largest of all cells is the ostrich egg, which is a little bigger than a grapefruit.

Most cells, however, are much too small to see without a microscope. A typical human cell, for instance, is so small that about 250 of them would fit on the period at the end of this sentence. The smallest human cell, the red blood cell, measures about 1/25,000th of an inch. That is, it would take twenty-five thousand of them to make a line one inch long. A typical plant cell is somewhat larger than a typical animal cell—about three times larger—but still too small to see with the naked eye.

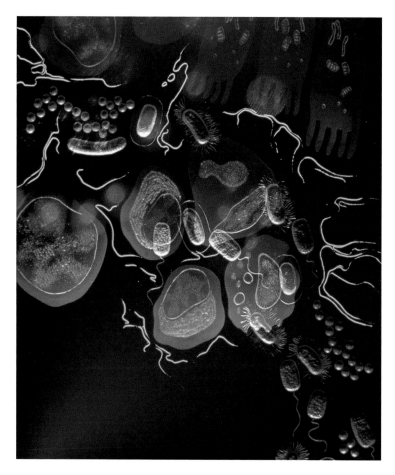

Cells come in many shapes and sizes.

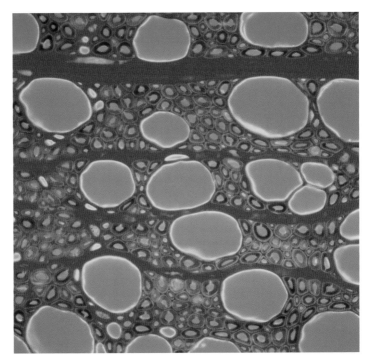

The cells of an oak leaf can be seen through a microscope.

A Single Cell

Some plants and animals consist of only one cell. Microscopic one-celled **organisms** live by the millions in pond water and in the ocean. A single drop of water may contain thousands of them.

One single-celled animal is the amoeba. The amoeba moves by extending a blob of itself in the direction it wants to go. These blobs are called pseudopods, or "false feet." The amoeba also sends out these false feet when it finds food. It "eats" by simply surrounding the food with its own body.

Another one-celled pond dweller is the paramecium, which is oval shaped. It is surrounded by a fringe of fine hairs called cilia. These hairs beat back and forth in a wavelike motion, moving the paramecium on its way through the water.

The very smallest and most primitive cells of all are the bacteria. They are so tiny that five hundred of them stacked on top of each other would rise no higher than the thickness of a dime. Scientists believe bacteria were probably the first forms of life to emerge on earth, probably almost 4 billion years ago. There are hundreds of thousands of different kinds of bacteria, and they live just about everywhere—in the ocean, in the soil, even in the human body.

Some bacteria cause disease but most do not affect human beings directly. The ones that do are not necessarily harmful. One kind of bacteria, for example, lives in human intestines. It helps to digest food, and it also produces certain vitamins. Bacteria live on the skin, too, millions of them on every square inch, without causing any harm.

Communities of Organisms

Some one-celled organisms join with others to form communities. Each cell in the community still carries on its independent life, finding food, eating, and reproducing. But cells that have gotten together can do things that cells alone cannot.

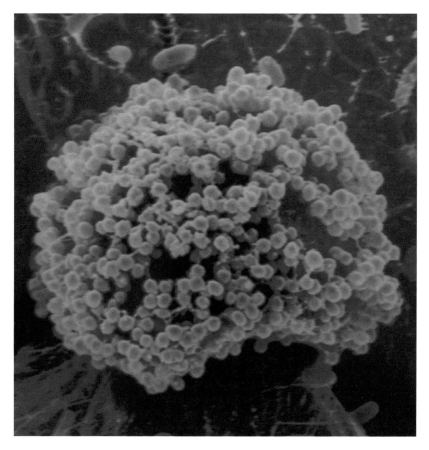

Tiny bacteria cells are among the simplest forms of life.

The slime mold, which lives on the forest floor, starts its life as an individual cell. On its own, it creeps across the ground, looking for food and eating it. When food becomes hard to find, however, the slime mold sends out a signal that calls to other slime molds. Thousands of them ooze toward the signal and join together to form something that looks like a slug about half an inch long. The "slug" crawls away to find food.

This "slug" is not really an animal, however, like a real slug. It has no mouth, no stomach, no head or tail. It is simply a community of single cells cooperating with each other. The community's purpose is to send out slime mold cells to new places where there might be more food. The slug crawls along until it reaches a high spot, such as the top of a log. There it sends up a stalk with a kind of bud on top. The bud bursts open, new one-celled slime molds are released, and they float out to new habitats. Then the cycle starts over again.

The volvox is another single-celled organism that forms communities. It lives in pond water. Each volvox cell has two tiny tails called flagellae that wave back and forth. Volvox cells, which are a beautiful green, group together in hollow spheres. Sometimes the spheres are made of thousands of cells. The biggest are one millimeter or more across and can be seen without a microscope.

The life-forms of the visible world—the plants in a garden, the trees in a forest, the insects and birds and other animals—are made up of far more cells than communities like that of the volvox, and their cells work together in a very different way.

Cells in Complex Organisms

A complex organism is an organized body of cells working together. This kind of organism is different in an important way from a simple community of cells. A community of cells, like the slime mold or the volvox, is made up of many cells that are all the same. A complex organism is made up of many different kinds of cells, all doing a part of the work that keeps the organism alive.

The plants and animals in the visible world are composed of vast numbers of cells. Some scientists estimate that in the body of an adult human being there might be 5 trillion cells. Others say the number is more like 60 trillion cells. That's more

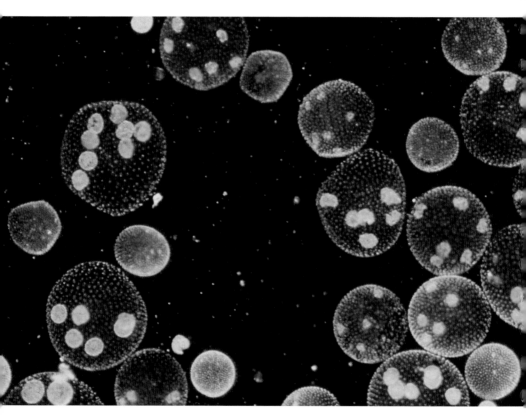

Volvox cells, seen here, live together in communities.

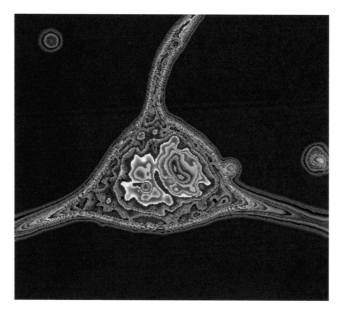

The nerve cell, pictured above, is one of the two hundred different kinds of cells in the human body.

cells than people on the earth—about eleven thousand times more.

The human body has about two hundred different kinds of cells. Among them are muscle cells, which make the body move; nerve cells, which carry messages to and from the brain; and skin cells, which form the body's protective covering. Blood cells, bone cells, lung and liver and hair cells—the work of all these cells is necessary for the health of the body.

Though cells are tiny, they work hard. As long as a cell is alive, it never stops working. In a way, cells are like tiny factories working to produce the energy of life twenty-four hours a day.

Chapter 2

How a Cell Works

Every cell, of every kind, is a living thing. The main job of a cell is the same as that of every living thing: to stay alive. Cells do that by taking in food and oxygen and changing it into energy for living—just as all plants and animals do. In recent years, scientists have been able to look inside of cells and see how they do this.

Seeing Inside a Cell

In the 1950s, scientists began to use electron microscopes to see the interior of cells. These powerful microscopes can magnify things up to a million times and give a picture of the details of a cell. But because of the way the electron microscope works, living cells cannot survive within it. So electron microscopes could view only dead cells.

Today scientists have found ways to combine microscopes with computers and video cameras to watch live cells in motion. They have found that cells are crowded, busy places, where a lot of activity is going on all the time. What happens inside a cell is so complex that scientists are only

The Cell

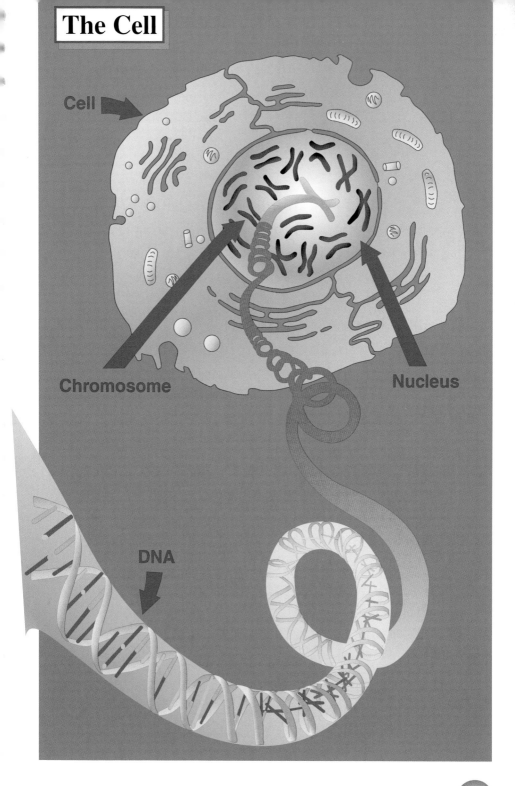

Cell

Chromosome

Nucleus

DNA

beginning to understand it. Some things are clear, though. One of them is that all cells have a kind of surrounding "skin"—a cell wall or cell membrane.

The Cell Wall

The cell wall or membrane surrounds the cell and keeps its contents inside. The walls of plant cells are fairly thick and stiff. The stiff cell walls help the plant keep its shape. Plant cells often look like small sharp-cornered rooms.

One easy way to see the walls of plant cells is to take a piece of the very thin tissue between the layers of an onion and look at it under a microscope. The onion cells are rectangular, like miniature shoe boxes. Most plant cells have this box-like, rigid shape.

The membrane of an animal cell is very thin—so thin that it is invisible under an ordinary microscope. It is also strong and flexible. If you could see a typical living animal cell magnified many thousands of times, it would look a bit like a balloon full of water. It would be moving—bulging out, shrinking back, pulsing with all the action inside it.

Cell walls are not solid like sheets of rubber, however. They are more like sieves, full of minute holes. The holes are actually "gateways" that will allow only oxygen and nutrients that the cell needs to pass through. Other such gateways allow wastes to flow out.

The Work of a Plant Cell

The cells that make up leaves and other green parts of plants contain tiny structures called **chloroplasts.** In a picture magnified many times, the chloroplasts would look like small green dots. Their purpose is to capture sunlight and use it to combine water and nutrients to make the energy the plant needs. This process is called **photosynthesis.**

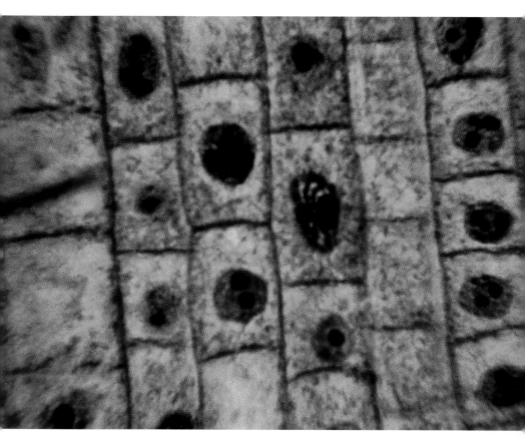

Chloroplasts trap sunlight, which plants need to grow.

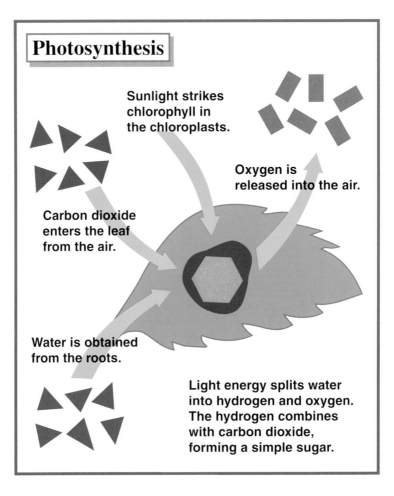

Photosynthesis

Sunlight strikes chlorophyll in the chloroplasts.

Oxygen is released into the air.

Carbon dioxide enters the leaf from the air.

Water is obtained from the roots.

Light energy splits water into hydrogen and oxygen. The hydrogen combines with carbon dioxide, forming a simple sugar.

During photosynthesis, water molecules are split apart. Water molecules consist of two hydrogen atoms and one oxygen atom. Once these have been broken apart, the cell uses the hydrogen and oxygen in different ways. It combines hydrogen with other things to make its food. It releases the oxygen into the air.

Almost all the oxygen that animals breathe comes from the photosynthesis going on in plant cells. Without the work of those tiny green chloro-plasts, life for human beings—and all other kinds of animals—would not be possible.

Animal Cells and Oxygen

All animal cells need oxygen to stay alive. If these cells do not get enough oxygen, they die. This is why living things must keep taking in air all the time—so that oxygen keeps traveling to all the cells of its body.

Blood cells (pictured) carry oxygen from the lungs to other cells in the body.

A cell gets oxygen through its cell wall or membrane. Oxygen from the air, or from water, passes through the gateways in the cell wall to the inside.

One-celled organisms are surrounded by air or water, so getting oxygen is simple: It comes in from all sides. Complex organisms have more complicated ways of getting oxygen. Many of the cells in a human body, for instance, are not in contact with the air. The cells of the stomach, the liver, and the heart are deep inside the body. Cells like these get their oxygen from the blood, which picks it up from the air in the lungs and carries it throughout the body in the blood vessels.

How Animal Cells Get Food

A cell needs food as well as oxygen. Food comes to the cell in the same way as oxygen, through the cell walls. But in order to pass through the cell walls, it must be broken down into very small pieces. This happens in the stomach and the digestive tract. From there, very small food molecules pass into the bloodstream and are carried all around the body. As the blood flows past the cells, the gateways in the cell wall recognize which nutrients the cell needs. It is a little like picking fish out of a stream. The gateways let in the molecules (including proteins, carbohydrates, and sugars) that the cell will use for making energy.

The Cell's Energy Factories

Just as a human body is filled with organs that do the work of life—such as the heart, the liver, and the lungs—each cell is filled with tiny **organelles** (the word just means "small organs"). Among these are the **mitochondria**, where molecules of food and oxygen are turned into energy. The mitochondria are like little power plants.

Some mitochondria are wormshaped or sausageshaped. Others are shaped more like blobs. Inside, the mitochondria are full of maze-like passages where the energy conversion is done.

Each cell contains a great many of these energy factories—hundreds or even thousands. They are constantly busy taking in food and oxygen and "burning" them together to make energy.

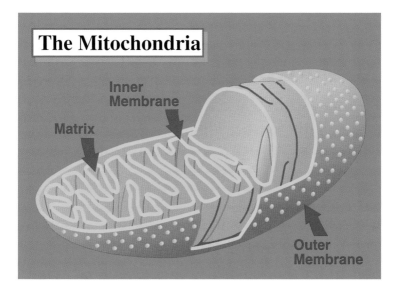

The Mitochondria

Inner Membrane

Matrix

Outer Membrane

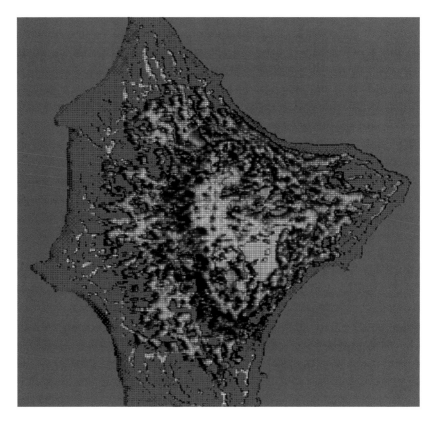

Skin cells serve as the body's protective covering. They try to keep harmful germs out.

Hard at Work

In a single-celled creature, or a community of single-celled creatures like the volvox, all the cells have the same job: to live and multiply. A complex organism such as a person, however, is made up of cells with many different kinds of work to do. The cells of the eyes do something different from the cells of the heart. The cells of the muscles do something different from the cells of the blood.

Cells have different shapes according to the kind of work they do. A human nerve cell, for instance, is long and stringlike. This is because the nerve cell carries signals from one part of the body to another. The nerve fibers that connect the toes to the spine can be nearly three feet long.

Skin cells, which form the body's protective outer covering, are flat. They form tight connections with each other. Their job is to hold in the body's fluids, to keep the body waterproof, and to keep harmful germs from getting in.

Red blood cells are among the smallest cells in the body. They are round and have a dent in the center. They look something like shallow bowls, or doughnuts with holes that don't go all the way through. Their size and shape allow them to flow easily through narrow blood vessels.

Another Big Job

By changing oxygen and food to energy, a cell accomplishes its first job: to stay alive and do the work it is designed for. But cells also have another crucial job: They must make new cells, so that the organism they are a part of can continue to live and grow. Deep inside the cell is the place where this begins.

Chapter 3

Cells Make More Cells

All living things have ways of making more of themselves. Plants make seeds that fall to the ground and sprout into new plants. Birds lay eggs that become new birds. Since cells are living things, they also reproduce. The process begins in a part of the cell called the **nucleus.**

The Nucleus

Inside nearly all kinds of cells is a nucleus. It is the biggest of the cell's organelles. In magnified pictures, the nucleus shows as a dark spot somewhere near the center of the cell.

The nucleus is the cell's command center. It holds the instructions that tell the cell what to do and when to do it. These instructions are contained in long, fine strings of molecules, coiled up and packed extremely tightly into the nucleus. If all of these strings were unwound and linked together, they would be about six feet long. This is an amazing length to be packed into such a small space. The

A scientist holds a model of a gene.

nucleus of a human cell is only 1/25,000th of an inch wide.

Along the strings of molecles are units called genes. Each gene holds one specific kind of instruction. The instructions within the genes determine everything about the cell—whether it is a human cell or a fish cell or a daisy cell; whether it is a brain cell or a blood cell; whether it is the cell of a person with red hair or the cell of a dog with blue eyes.

The instructions within a gene also tell the cell how to make more cells. That process begins in the nucleus.

How a Cell Divides

Suppose a scientist is looking at a chicken cell through a powerful microscope. The nucleus of the cell looks like a shadowy dot. But as the scientist watches, a change takes place in the nucleus. Small dark shapes appear. They form pairs and arrange themselves in a line. What has happened is that the genetic material in the nucleus has bunched together into little rod-shaped "packages" called **chromosomes.** There are twenty-three pairs of chromosomes in human beings.

Next, the pairs begin to separate. They pull away from each other. The cell walls, too, pull outward farther and farther. Finally, the cell splits in half and two new cells are formed. Both have exactly the same chromosomes. One cell has become two cells.

The cells in a person's body are dividing all the time. Every second, about 10 million cell divisions take place. Some kinds of cells divide faster than others. The cells of the intestine divide the fastest. Skin cells divide quickly, too, making new cells to replace old ones that flake away. A person has an entirely new skin about once a month.

How an Organism Grows

Every living thing begins life as a single cell. The single cell divides and becomes two cells. Each of those cells divides, and the result is four cells.

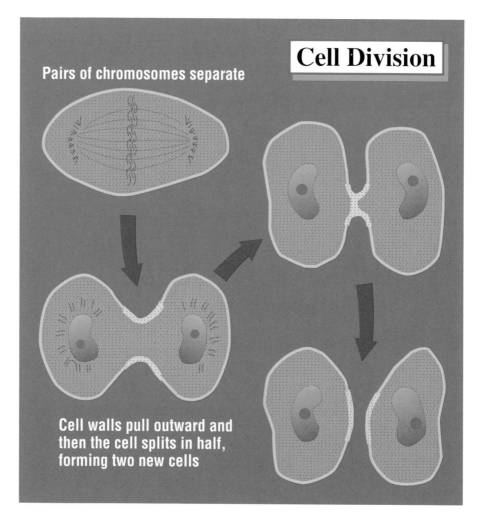

Cell Division

Pairs of chromosomes separate

Cell walls pull outward and then the cell splits in half, forming two new cells

Another division, and there are eight cells—and so on, until the organism is a ball of cells.

In simple organisms like the volvox, made up of all one kind of cell, cells continue to divide in this same way, making more and more identical cells. But a complex organism is made up of many different kinds of cells. Eventually some cells must become bone cells, some must become muscle cells, and some must become blood cells. That is, the cells must specialize.

The information contained in the genes tells the cells how to do this, and when. In a human being, the cells begin to differentiate after they have been dividing for about ten days. At this point, they have formed a hollow ball. From here on, they will take one of three paths. The cells on the outside of the ball will become the outer parts of the body, such as the skin. Cells in the middle layer will become such things as bones, muscles, and blood vessels. And cells on the inner layer will

Cells divide to form new life.

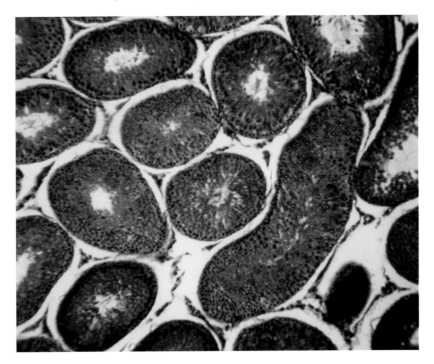

form the organs, such as the heart and liver. As the dividing goes on, the cells will become more and more specialized, until there are cells for everything from eyebrows to toenails.

Knowing What to Do

When a liver cell divides, it makes more liver cells. When a skin cell divides, it makes more skin cells. Each kind of cell can only make copies of itself. It can't do anything else. But all the cells in a body contain *the same* **genes** that were in the body's very first cell. These genes gave instructions for building all the parts of the body. Scientists have been puzzled by this question: If all cells in a body contain a complete set of instructions, how do cells "know" to become skin cells, muscle cells, or any other kind?

The answer seems to be that genes are something like switches that can be turned on and off. When a cell begins to specialize, some of its genes are turned off. If it is going to be an outer layer cell, then the genes for making the middle and inner layers are turned off. Those genes are still there in the nucleus of the cell. But from then on, the cell doesn't use them. As it becomes more and more specialized, more and more of its genes are turned off, until only the ones that make it what it's supposed to be—a brain cell, a red blood cell, a cell of the eye—are available.

Regeneration

Some cells seem to know how to reproduce themselves in a remarkable way. When a lizard loses its tail, for example, the cells in the tail's stump very soon begin to multiply and form a new tail. The salamander can do something even more amazing: If it loses a leg, it can grow a new one, toes and all.

Human bodies can't do this. If a person loses a finger, no new finger—complete with bones, nerves, and skin—will grow in its place. Human cells know how to make copies of themselves only. Skin cells will make new skin cells to cover a wound, and liver cells can often make more liver cells to repair a damaged or lost part of the liver. But once a human baby is formed, its cells seem to "forget" how to make an arm or a leg.

Cells Live and Die

As well as knowing what kind of cell to become, cells know how long to live. Some kinds of cells live only for a short time. Certain white blood cells, for example, live for only a few days. Other kinds of cells live for the entire life of the organism. Most of a person's brain cells live as long as the person does. A very elderly person could have brain cells nearly a hundred years old.

A young body grows because its cells are dividing, making more and more cells to add to bones,

A person who loses a finger cannot grow a new one.

muscles, and skin. An adult body stops growing. Its cells are still dividing, but most of them are not adding to the total number of cells in the body. They are replacing cells that die and doing other important jobs.

How long to live, whether to divide, how often to divide—all these are programmed into the cell's genes. In a healthy body, the cells are all doing what they're supposed to do—billions of them, working hard and on schedule. It's an amazingly complicated process and very difficult to understand. But the more scientists learn about the lives of cells, the more they are learning about the lives of people, both in health and in illness.

Cells in Health and Illness

Certain cells can cause a great deal of trouble in the human body. Other cells have the job of defending us against that trouble. Whether a body is ill or healthy depends on whether the harmful cells or the helpful cells have the upper hand.

Cells That Defend and Heal

The white blood cells have the job of protecting the human body. There are several different kinds of white blood cells. Together, they make up a defending army known as the **immune system.**

The first job of the immune system is to decide what belongs in the body and what doesn't. The "soldiers" of the immune system are very skillful at recognizing invaders such as harmful bacteria. If a splinter gets under the skin, for example, bringing bacteria with it, one of these cells sounds the alarm, and the immune system springs into action.

The first to arrive are the **phagocytes.** These are large cells that have one job: to "eat" any dangerous organisms before they can divide and multiply. Phagocytes are constantly wandering around the body, gobbling up anything that doesn't belong there. When a foreign thing such as a splinter invades, they rush to the site. The redness and soreness of the skin around a cut, and the pus that sometimes gathers there, are signs that the phagocytes are at work.

White blood cells fight off germs that make people sick.

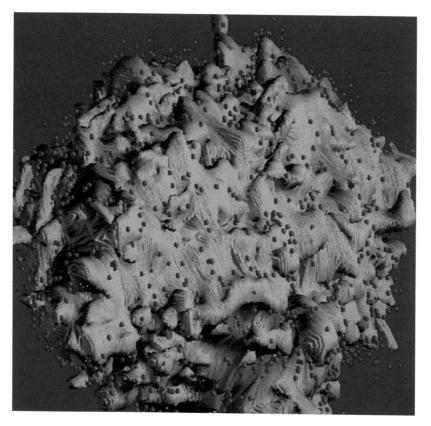

Some invaders make it past the phagocytes. Then the next line of defenders comes into play. These are the **lymphocytes,** another kind of white blood cell. Some of these are "killer" cells that destroy invading organisms by punching holes in their cell walls. Others make chemicals called **antibodies** that latch on to the outside of harmful organisms and hold them until the killer cells can destroy them.

Threats to Health

The immune system is not foolproof. Sometimes the body is attacked by viruses or bacteria the immune system can't handle. Fast-growing cancer cells can overwhelm the immune system. And sometimes the immune system itself goes awry and attacks the cells of the body.

Harmful bacteria and viruses can get into the body in several ways. They can enter when the skin is cut or punctured. They can come in when a person eats spoiled food. People can drink them in water or breathe them in. Once harmful bacteria or viruses get into the bloodstream or other body fluids, they can cause many kinds of diseases, from minor ones such as colds to serious ones such as malaria, meningitis, and tetanus.

Invaders from outside the body are not the only thing that can cause disease. Sometimes something goes wrong with the body's *own* cells. For

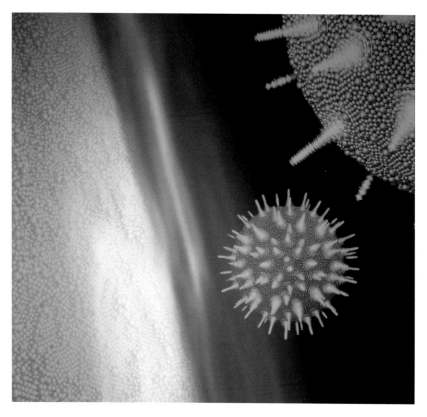

Human cells cannot defend themselves against attacks by some viruses, like this AIDS virus.

reasons scientists don't entirely understand, the genetic material in a cell can change, or **mutate,** in such a way that the cell no longer works as it should. The result can be a serious illness.

Cells with the Wrong Shape

One such illness is sickle-cell anemia. The red blood cells of people who have this disease contain a mutated gene. Normal red blood cells are round,

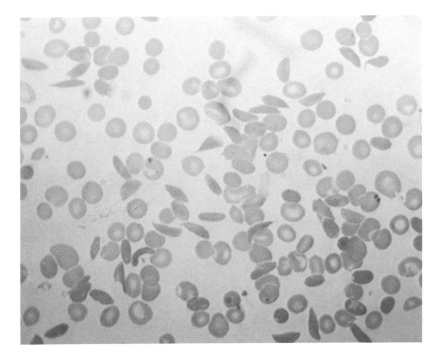

Sickle-shaped cells are a sign of disease.

like little saucers, and they are soft and flexible so that they can flow easily through even the tiniest blood vessels. But in a person with sickle-cell anemia, the damaged gene causes some of the blood cells to be shaped like sickles. (A sickle is a sharp, curved tool used for cutting tall grass.) These sickle-shaped cells catch and stick together, clogging narrow blood vessels. People with sickle-cell anemia, which is most common among those of African descent, suffer severe pain. Because their blood can't carry oxygen easily to all parts of the body, they are weak and open to infections. They usually die from the disease.

Cells That Keep Growing

Cancer is another disease that results from cells in which genetic materials mutate in a harmful way. Normal cells die after they have divided a certain number of times. But cancer cells have lost the part of their instructions that says "stop." They keep on dividing, and the multiplying cells form a mass that is called a **tumor.**

Cancer cells don't look like ordinary cells. They are often larger, and their nucleus takes up more of the space inside. They have an irregular shape, and they

A computer image of a brain tumor (in red) inside a person's skull.

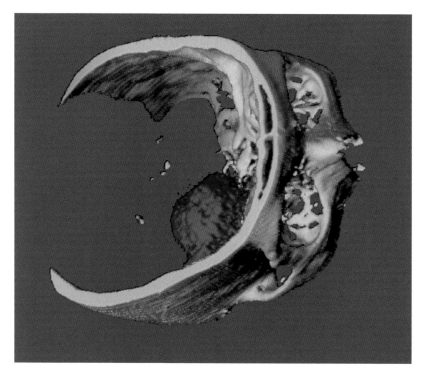

come together not in the neat patterns that healthy cells make but in an untidy, scrambled mass.

Many different kinds of cells can become cancerous. The ones that do so most often are the cells that divide most often, such as skin cells. This is because with every division, a cell must make a copy of its genes, and the more often it does this, the more chance there is for something to go wrong. Skin cancers are very common. Cancers that affect the nerve cells, which don't divide, are very uncommon.

Scientists know some of the reasons why cells become cancerous. Very poisonous chemicals can cause it, such as the ones in tobacco smoke and certain pesticides. Too much radiation, from the sun or other sources, can cause cells to turn cancerous. Doctors have ways of killing cancer cells, but most of these ways make the patient feel very ill and cause problems such as hair loss. Scientists are looking for ways to attack cancer cells without harming healthy cells.

Cells That Attack the Body

Sometimes the body turns against itself. The cells of the immune system seem to mistake the body's own tissues for foreign invaders. They fight against them, causing pain and inflammation. This is what happens in rheumatoid arthritis, for

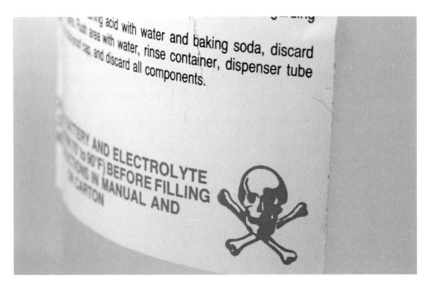

Cigarettes and some pesticides can harm cells.

instance. The body's immune system attacks the tissue of its own joints.

Scientists do not yet know why a person's immune system cells sometimes attack that person's own body. It is just one of the many mysteries that remain to be solved about how illnesses are caused and cured. But the study of how cells work is providing some new answers.

New Knowledge, New Hopes

In recent years, scientists have been studying the genes that lie in the nucleus of every cell. Some scientists have been part of a tremendous project: to figure out what each one of the approximately 80,000 human genes does. The gene for sickle-cell

Scientists study genes to learn ways of keeping people healthy.

anemia has already been identified. So has the gene that causes muscular dystrophy, a disease that makes muscles become weak and useless. If there were a way to repair those genes or to replace them with healthy genes, those diseases could be wiped out.

New knowledge about cancer cells may also offer hope. Cancer cells are often able to "hide" from the immune system. They can disguise themselves with chemicals that make them seem like normal body cells. Scientists are looking for a way to help the cells of the immune system recognize cancer cells so they can fight against them.

Researchers are also studying cell **regeneration.** One of their goals is to find a way to make damaged nerve cells regenerate. This could help the many people who are paralyzed by accidents to their spinal cords.

People with badly damaged hearts, livers, or kidneys often need to have their damaged organs replaced with new ones in order to stay alive. The best doctors can do for these people now is to give them an organ transplant—that is, to replace the damaged organ with an organ from someone who has died. But this can cause problems. The cells of the immune system see the new organ as a foreign

The study of cells offers much hope for the future.

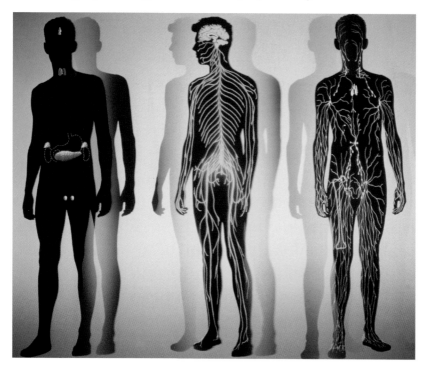

body. They attack it and try to destroy it, and they often succeed. Many transplanted organs are rejected in this way.

This problem could be solved if scientists could use the patient's own cells to grow new organs—if they could take a healthy cell from a patient's heart, for instance, and use it to grow a new heart, as a lizard grows a new tail. So far, this has not been possible, though some scientists think it can be done.

The human cells that regenerate most easily are skin cells. Scientists are looking for ways to take skin cells from a burned patient and use them to grow new skin in the laboratory. Doctors could then use these pieces of new skin to heal the patient's burns. Because the original skin cells came from the patient, the patient's immune system would not attack them.

Into the Future

The tiny world of the cell is full of mysteries and marvels. Scientists have been studying the cell for a long time, but only in the last few years have they begun to learn the secrets of the genes. This knowledge will open many possibilities in the years ahead. Already, the end of some genetic diseases may be in sight. As scientists learn more and more about the building blocks of life, other changes will come, too, and they are likely to be profound and surprising.

Glossary

antibodies: Chemicals in some white blood cells that help to protect against invading bacteria and viruses.

chloroplasts: Structures in plant cells that convert sunlight into energy.

chromosomes: Small "packages" that genes form into when a cell is about to divide.

genes: Long strings of molecules packed into the nucleus of a cell. They are the cell's instructions.

immune system: The "army" of white blood cells that defends the body against harmful invaders.

lymphocytes: A kind of white blood cell in the immune system.

mitochondria: The "power plants" inside the cell, where food and oxygen are converted into energy.

mutate: To change. Some diseases are caused by genetic material that has mutated.

nucleus: The "command center" of a cell. It holds the genes, the cell's instructions.

organelles: Tiny structures within a cell.

organism: An organized community of cells, such as a plant or animal.

phagocytes: White blood cells that "eat" harmful bacteria.

photosynthesis: The process by which a plant converts sunlight into food and energy.

regeneration: The ability to grow new cells to replace damaged ones; especially, to grow a new body part, as a lizard grows a new tail.

tumor: A mass of cells, sometimes cancerous.

Books

Dr. Fran Balkwill, *Cells Are Us*. Minneapolis: Carolrhoda Books, 1993. A simple, illustrated look at the cells that make up a human being.

Nina Canault, *Incredibly Small: Frontiers of the Invisible*. New York: New Discovery Books, 1993. Pictures taken with a scanning electron microscope, showing insects, cells, computer chips, and plants in amazing detail.

Mahlon Hoagland and Bert Dodson, *The Way Life Works: Everything You Need to Know About the Way All Life Grows, Develops, Reproduces, and Gets Along*. New York: Times Books, 1995. Illustrated with lively cartoons, this book includes chapters about the workings of the cell, DNA, and cell communities.

The Incredible Voyage: Exploring the Human Body. Washington, DC: National Geographic Society, 1998. A large book full of wonderful pictures, including a great many taken with advanced microscopes. Includes good information on the human body and medical advances.

Patricia M. Kelly, *The Mighty Human Cell*. New York: John Day, 1967. Easy-to-understand descriptions, with drawings, of the different kinds of human cells.

Stephen P. Kramer, *Getting Oxygen*. New York: Thomas Y. Crowell, 1986. How cells get the oxygen necessary for their survival.

Donald M. Silver, *One Small Square Pond.* New York: W. H. Freeman, 1994. The life in a woodland pond, explored with illustrations and experiments to try.

Georg Zappler, *From One Cell to Many Cells.* New York: Julian Messner, 1970. The development of a human being from a single cell.

Websites

Cells Alive (www.cellsalive.com). This site shows pictures of different kinds of cells taken with an electron microscope. There are also short "movies" showing cells in motion. You can see how a bacteria "swims" and how a cell "eats" an invading bacteria. Clear explanations go with the pictures.

Dennis Kunkel's Microscopy (www.pbrc.hawaii.edu/~kunkel). Pictures taken with a scanning electron microscope provide a colorful view of the world too small to be seen with the naked eye. Includes pictures of many different kinds of cells and also insects, fish scales, fungus, spiders, and more.

How Stuff Works (www.howstuffworks.com/cell.htm). This site explains, in simple language, many aspects of cell biology.

Robert Hooke (www.roberthooke.org.uk). A picture of the drawing Robert Hooke made of the cork cells he saw in the microscope. Title page from his famous work *Micrographia.*

Index

amoebas, 8
animals
  cells of
    food and, 20
    oxygen and, 19–20
    walls of, 16
  single-celled, 8–9, 20
  see also human cells

bacteria, 9, 34
blood cells
  food and, 20
  life of, 30
  oxygen and, 20
  red
    shape of, 23
    sickle-cell anemia and,
      35–36
    sizes of, 7
  white, 32
  see also immune system
buds, 11

cancer cells
  disguises used by, 40
  immune system and, 34
  shapes of, 37–38
cells
  division of
    cancer cells and, 38
    described, 26–27
    specialization and, 27–29

sizes of, 6–7
walls of, 16, 20
see also specific cell types
chloroplasts, 17
chromosomes, 26
cork, 4–5

eggs, 6

food
  amoebas and, 8
  animal cells and, 20
  mitochondria and, 21
  slime molds and, 10–11

genes
  cancer cells and, 37
  changes in, 35
  as instructions, 25, 29, 31
  muscular dystrophy and,
    40
  number of, 39
  sickle-cell anemia and,
    35–36, 39–40
  specialization and, 28
  as switches, 29

Hooke, Robert, 4–5
human cells
  number of, 12
  sizes of, 6–7
  types of, 13

immune system
  attacks body, 38–39
  cancer cells and, 34, 40
  invasion of, 32, 34–35
  lymphocytes and, 34
  organ transplants and, 41
  phagocytes and, 33
  white blood cells and, 32

lymphocytes, 34

membranes, 16, 20
microscopes, 4, 14
mitochondria, 21
molds, 10–11
muscular dystrophy, 40

nerve cells, 23
nucleus, 24–25

organelles, 21, 24
organisms
  communities of, 9–11, 12
  complex, 11–13
organ transplants, 41
oxygen
  animal cells and, 19–20
  mitochondria and, 21
  plant cells and, 18–19
  sickle-cell anemia and, 36

paramecium, 9
phagocytes, 33
photosynthesis, 17–19
plant cells
  photosynthesis and, 17–19
  shapes of, 16
  sizes of, 7
  walls of, 16
pseudopods, 8

regeneration, 30, 41
reproduction
  cancer cells and, 38
  described, 26–27
  specialization and, 27–29
rheumatoid arthritis,
  38–39

shapes, 23, 35–36
sickle-cell anemia
  gene for, 39–40
  red blood cells and,
    35–36
skin cells, 23, 42
slime molds, 10–11

tumors, 37

viruses, 34
volvox, 11